The Last Sip: A Coffee-Stained Eulogy (A Poetic Memoir of Love)

Garima Singh

BookLeaf Publishing

India | USA | UK

Presentation by *BookLeaf Publishing*

Web: www.bookleafpub.com

E-mail: info@bookleafpub.com

ISBN: 9789360949365

First edition 2024

To the Coffee Devotees and the Casual Sippers Alike:

This collection is dedicated to each and every one of you. Whether your mornings begin with the energising aroma of a freshly brewed cup or your coffee experience is more occasional, these poems resonate with the universal language of love, loss and the resilience of the human spirit.

And to Those Who Have Loved, Lost and Still Stand Strong:

You are a testament to the enduring power of the heart. This book is a celebration of your strength, a reminder that even in the face of loss, love leaves an indelible mark.

Remember You Are Special:

Never forget that even amidst love's embrace, heartbreak's sting or life's inevitable losses, your inner light continues to shine. You are special, not because of external circumstances but because of the love that resides within you.

PREFACE

The first sip ignites a memory; the last one leaves a bittersweet echo. *In The Last Sip: A Coffee-Stained Eulogy*, coffee isn't just a drink; it's a portal to a life richly woven with love, loss and the quiet strength found in shared moments. This collection delves into a true story, its details veiled in a touch of mystery, yet the emotions resonate with a universal truth.

These poems explore the symphony of life played out over countless cups of coffee. You'll encounter the nervous anticipation of a first date fuelled by caffeine's warmth, the comforting routine of shared mornings and the raw ache of loss that lingers with every sip. Here, amidst the bittersweet fragrance, you'll find the echoes of laughter and tears, the sting of absence and the flickering ember of hope that refuses to be extinguished.

'The Last Sip' is an invitation to embark on a journey of introspection. As you turn the pages, prepare to revisit your own memories, the ones steeped in the aroma of coffee. This collection is a celebration of love's enduring power, a testament to the resilience of the human spirit.

So, pour yourself a cup of your favourite brew, settle in and allow these poems to transport you. You might just find a piece of your own story reflected within these pages.

Cappuccino Crush
(The First Glance)

Sun spills through stained glass, a Sunday prism,
A hidden café, a solace from the city's schism.
He enters, book in hand, a paperback old,
Tall and lean, hair as dark as midnight's hold.

Across the chamber, she glides with grace,
In flowing ivory, a floral embrace.
Maxi dress dancing on the breeze,
Hair in a bun, mind at ease.

They choose separate seats, worlds unknown,
Yet in their own tales, each soul is prone.
Verbs consume; his mind in a lettered tide,
She, lost in her thoughts, a gaze veiled inside.

Cappuccino sings, the grinder's gentle hum,
A harmonious duet, a rhythm well-strum.
Bound eyes meet in a seraphic glance,
A calming, wordless trance across the expanse.

Beans pirouette, an aromatic, swirling storm,
Sweetness chases bitterness, a brewing form.
Nervous fingers tighten, a blush upon her cheek,
He ducks back to his story, words he can't speak.

Steamed and frothed, a shimmery, milky crown,
A flicker in their irises, a spark, then quickly
down.
The world fades out in the cafe's gentle din,
Lost in silence, a connection wants to begin.

Cups clink, frothy goblets, enigmatic dreams,
The first sip, a saga yet to be inscribed on life's
satin seams.
A sideswipe peep, a missed dart, hesitant, shy,
Then fate intervenes, a phone rings with a cry.

She gathers up her world, his heart inside,
A wish for something more, a future, wide.
He witnesses her departure, a forced valediction,
The vacant chalice rests, evaporating affection.

Like spent coffee grounds clinging to porcelain's hold,
A tenacious longing in the kernels of his spirit did enfold.
The empty cappuccino cup, a canvas now bare,
Awaits swirling languidly, to be painted there.

Galao Gambit
(Taking the Chance)

All week, a fumbled foxtrot, Sunday, their
sonata,
Would fate reunite them, a gambit to be played.
He ironed every shirt, a quest for flawlessness,
His heart – a nervous Galao, emotions in a mess.

She whirled, a flurry of chiffon, her confidante,
a style guru,
'Dress or bodice, brazen or coy, a siren's call or
hushed allure'?
'Seductive mystique or polished grace'? her
brow furrowed in dismay,
For hearts entangled, it seemed, a sartorial ballet
held sway.

Brushes twirled and mascara, a warrior's paint
and plume,
Hair teased to perfect chaos, dispelling basement
gloom.
He pondered in the shower, a steam-filled, soapy
dance,
Emerging wrinkled pink, a love-struck,
prune-like chance.

His mind, like the Galao, a tempestuous brew,
Mirrored the clash of emotions, both vibrant and
blue.
The milk, like her softness, the coffee, his
resolve steep,
A perfect, balanced mixture, a bond he strove to
keep.

He pushed through the cafe door, an eagle, eyes
alight,
Each table was filled with strangers, not the girl
in his sight.
Disappointment's bitter sting, a cold and
creeping dread,
Had fate, the fickle jester, turned his heart
instead?

Her twinkles swept the familiar scene, a
nervous, butterfly chase,
Empty chairs and steaming mugs, a vacant,
sunlit space.
Blaze flickered, then diminished, a fragile flame
that died,
Had she misread the signals? Did in guarded
glances he lied?

But then, a voice, a stammer, a familiar, nervous
hum,
'Excuse me, is this seat…'? Their eyes, a joyful
thrum.
A smile, a blush, a fumbled word – the ice began
to melt,
For on that sunlit Sunday, a Galao bond found a
chance to dwelt.

Mocha Mischief
(A Nervous Reunion)

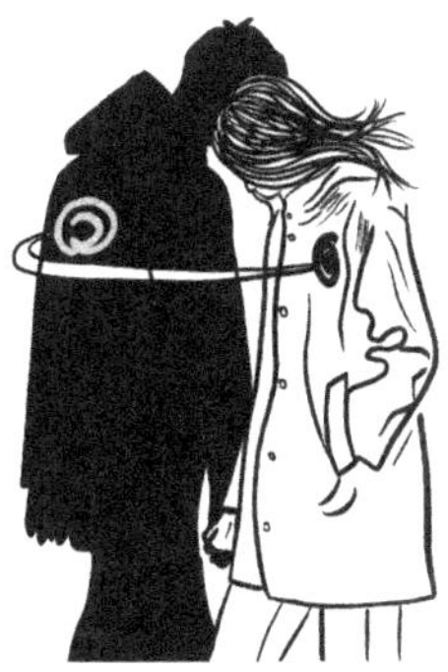

His mind, a mocha muddle, whipped with
anxious delight,
He spun around the cafe, a crowded, sunlit bite.
There, her gaze met his, seeking empty
sweetness, lit by romance,
A shot of joyous espresso, a nervous, awkward
glance.

A radiant smile, a flourish of ethereal froth,
powerless to restrain,
Surrendered then to an abyss of bitterness, an
unknown, unspoken strain.
The cafe, a grinding turmoil with nowhere to
retreat,
They waited, hearts like brewing grounds, for
destiny to meet.

He choked on a dry breath, a hesitant 'Hello',
Her cheeks flushed like roses, her voice soft and
slow...
Words tumbled, tangled grounds, thrumming
with hidden dread,
Whispers choked, emotions raw, a silent plea left
unaddressed.

The moments dripped like coffee, a crowded,
swirling stream,
A stranger filled the table; their conversation – a
dream.
A silent fight brewed fiercely, a battle nerves
ignite,
To bridge the cocoa chasm, a connection takes
flight.

A comrade's touch, a sudden loss of the fire's
gentle sway,
A parting blink, a shadow cast upon a wonderful
day.
No numbers exchanged, a hopeful, 'See you
next week, perhaps'?
A shared, unspoken sadness, like fading froth,
collapses.

They walked out to the routine, a question in
their eyes,
Would they reconnect beneath those Sunday
skies?
The cafe held this envelope, a silent witness
perched upon the shelf,
Two souls who craved a mocha pause, a tale yet
to unfurl itself.

Con Panama Match
(A Sweet Beginning)

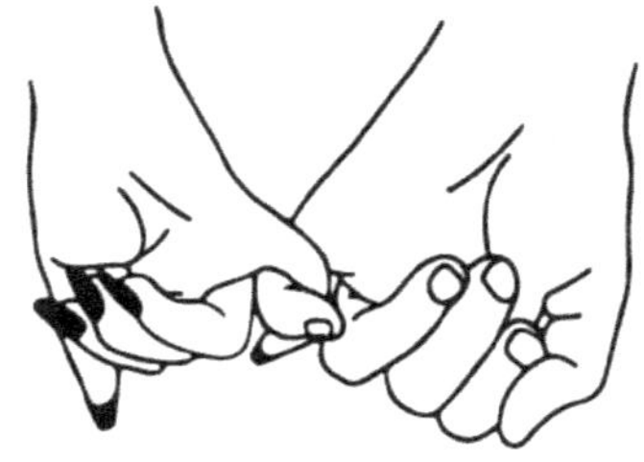

Empty Sundays, a taut bowstring, a lingering
inanition's sting,
Hope's fragile warmth like frothy drowning
foam, a Sisyphean climb to cling.
Eyes scanned the room, a name on trembling
lips,
But only strangers sat, with indifferent sips.

Then, a Friday night, a twist so keen,
He found a familiar face, bathed in the cafe's
midnight sheen.
Shock and surprise, a jolt like espresso's might,
A hushed supplication met with an ambrosial
delight.

No silences lingered, no time to let it cool,
He stepped forward, with his heart swinging full.
'Hi', he offered, a hopeful refrain,
Her pearls of white in reply, erasing all that pain.

'May I join you'? he asked, voice alight,
'Yes, please do', a welcome, oh so bright!
Worn volumes swapped, kindred spirits align,
Keats' odes and Coelho's magic entwine.

Music intertwined, a tarantella in their ears,
Rock's vibrant energy, classical's calming years.
'Coke Studio too'! she exclaimed, an infectious
grin,
His laughter reverberated, a light, cheerful
scene.

Hours flew by, a cafe's comforting hum,
Conversations flowed, free as endless cream's
sum.
Con Panamanian sipped, a nectar so rare,
Symbiotically paints the connection, spark
beyond compare.

A heady fragrance drooled, an alluring paradox,
The first sip, a cascade of sweetness, a
harmonious accord.
Numbers exchanged, a connection taking flight,
This acquaintance encounter, mixing of milk in
coffee so right.

A parting laced with tenderness, a wordless pact
held tight,
Their gazes, eloquent poems, words unspoken
flying like a kite.
Her Con Panamanian's essence, a sweet,
unforgettable trace,
A reminder of fate's intervention, as a blanket in
a winter place.

Latte Brushstrokes
(Painting Her Essence)

Text messages pinged with silly song quotes,
Emojis and questions in blossoming notes.
Simple greetings, a sunrise's gentle chime,
Good morning rituals exchanged over time.

As the phone calls stretched, a celestial tapestry
billowed,
Companionship bloomed in hushed moments, a
nascent world.
Precious 'goodnights' exchanged, a dreamy
sigh,
The phone clicks dead, and a latte dream talks of
muse in his eye.

Her beauty, a sunbeam's playful twerk, an allure
that can't be denied,
A whimsical artistry, a captivating delight, as her
laughter's vibrant tide.

Her smile, a burst of sunshine, sugar-sweet and
bright,
Make my own lips curve in a string of
dewdrops, transparent and light.

Hair like latte foam, soft and frothy, I yearn,
To bury my face in that cloud, a comfort yet to
be earned.
Cheeks, oh those cheeks, like a latte's fluffy
cloud,
A tenderness blooming, a secret desire avowed.

Eyes, deep and trenchant, like espresso's bold
brew,
Reflecting emotions, honest and as pellucid as
crystals.
She understands me, the way milk and coffee
meet,
A perfect blend, an estuary where river and
ocean greet.

She stirs like warm latte art, a vision so surreal,
Her laughter, a treasure, a sparkling, joyful peal.
A hug, a latte's comfort on a cold, wintry scene,
Melting away worries with a sonorous lull so
serene.

Holding her hand, a feeling that soothes like a
gentle breeze,
A secure anchor, an affection that brings me
inner ease.
Now, without her voice, a craving takes root,
A caffeine addiction, a dependence absolute.

Just as latte art, a Picasso on porcelain's rim,
Releases creatures fantastical in a frothy, playful
whim.
Creamy curves cascade, a form both bold and
sweet,
A reflection of her beauty, oh so complete.

Espresso Martini Muse
(The Swirl of his Charm)

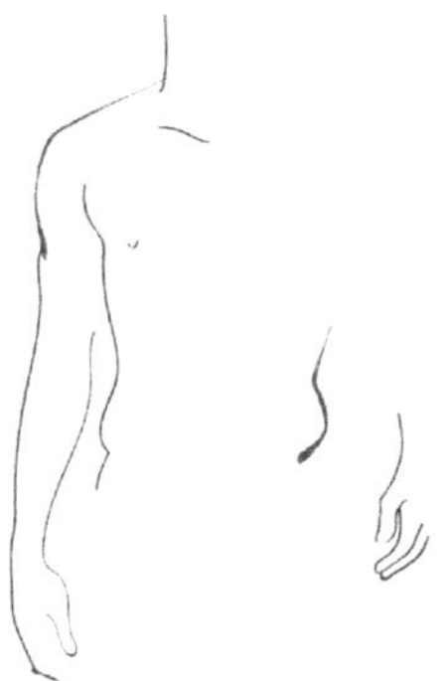

The phone, a familiar ember, pressed close
against her cheek,
His voice, a songbird's call, a rhythm both sharp
and meek.
He surpassed imaginings, a sculpted ideal
brought forth,
Dark eyes that scintillate, brimming with joyous
mirth.

Hair like espresso beans, rich and dark,
Curly tendrils mirroring my tangled spark.
Thoughts and desires, a whirlwind in bloom,
His presence calms me, dispels all gloom.

His eyes, oh his eyes, a roasted coffee bean's
gleam,
Pierce through my facade, a hushing, unspoken
dream.
Yet, a childish giddiness bubbles within,
A wild, alluring allemande, a desire to begin.

His gaze, a vodka shot, sharp and true,
Igniting a fire, a sensation so new.
It burns through defences, a welcome surprise,
A yearning to delve deeper into his mesmerising
eyes.

His smile, a crescent moon carved from pure
delight,
Dissolving anxieties that clung through the
night.
A wilted flower, parched and brown with woe,
His presence, a life-giving rain to make the
beauty flow.

His words, like Kahlua, deep and intense,
Spark philosophical debates, a world without a
fence.
Complex and vehement, they leave a lasting
trace,
Unravelling mysteries, like untangling a knotted
thread's lace.

His utterances, a cascade of syrupy balm,
Imbued with an aura of inviolability, quieting
inner alarms.
Amidst life's frenetic choreography, a fervent
desire I possess,
A tacit vow of solace, a sanctuary yet to
manifest.

The Espresso Martini, a tempest in a glass,
A bitter symphony where tensions amass.
Each feature a facet, a flavour yet to name,
Like finding faces in a clouded sky, a captivating
game.

Café Breve Bond
(The Perfect Blend)

In that selfsame café, where fate's hand
intervened,
Their fingers intertwined – a fresh narrative yet
unseen.
Words cascaded like a dulcet aria, tranquil and
pure,
Each ephemeral glimpse, a crimson tide, a
forbidden allure.

Mezzo e Mezzo dreams, like froth upon a gilded
cup,
Understanding blossoms, bathed in the cafe's
gentle sup.
Secret nicknames shared, spoken with delight,
An incipient alliance, a destiny burning ever so
bright.

Cafe Breve arrives, a welcome respite,
Warmth in their touch, a beautiful sight.
Steamy sips entwined, a contented sigh,
Sweetness surrounds them, beneath a gentle sky.

He, the bold espresso shot, a fire in his eyes,
Speaks of adventures, a future that flies.
She, the essence of milk, a spirit calm and kind,
Listens with a tender smile, a heart with purpose
aligned.

Their words ignite a vibrant spark, a captivating
display,
Opposing sides, they may embark on, yet hearts
are drawn this way.
His audacious spirit, a conflagration bright,
Her serene demeanour, a rest in the murk of
night.

Cafe Breve speaks, a metaphor so clear,
Two halves combining, dispelling all fear.
Resembling stratified richness, a flawless
configuration,
Their contrasts meld a fusion that intertwines.

Café Breve, a celestial dream, swirls in their sight,
A creamy nebula, bathed in ethereal light.
This haven, their sanctuary, a consortium brought to life,
Each whisper of Breve, a shared purpose to feel alive.

Mazagran Magic
(The Brewed Kiss)

Sun-bathed laughter spills and swirls, the cafe's
lively space,
Mazagran's citrussy delight, a playful, tangy
chase.
Ice cubes chime a flirtatious tune, a tableau so
sweet,
Their gazes entwine, a murmured sonnet, a tie
they can't retreat.

Bitter brew's aroma, a thrill that sends a blush,
Subtle gazes, yearning deep, a hidden, burning
crush.
Words like fireflies, they rapture and tease, a
playful disguise,
A blush that betrays, a story it spills in the
depths of their mesmerised eyes.

Conversations flow like honeyed wine; a spark
ignites the air,
Electricity crackles, leaving shivers everywhere.
Flirty touches linger, a brush of hand on hand,
A jolt that sends a current through, across the
promised land.

Hanker limned within their gaze, a silent, soulful
plea,
Hearts pound a frantic, rhythmic beat, a toccata
for thee.
Distance shrinks, dissolves with ease, dispelling
every fear,
Hesitation fades, a breath held tight, uncaging all
the gears.

Closed eyes meet, a tender touch, lips softly
come alive,
Mazagran's magic, rum-kissed tide, where
dreams and futures thrive.
Fingers interlace, a silent pact forged, a destiny
veiled in veins,
A narrative inscribed with vibrant hues, a
verdant scene.

The moment deepens, a burning want, the lips
blowing the fire,
Tongues meet in battle – a sweet surprise, a
passion that takes higher.
Refractive lime, a sharpness that dances in their
irisé,
The world blurs softly, a humming current, a
paradise that hypnotises.

Moonlight spills, a silver sheet on caged
fingertips,
Promises bloom unspoken, where every silence
drips.
Citrussy zest surrenders to an ambered
incandescence,
Mazagran music orchestrates a frenzied,
impassioned chase.

Café Brulot's Blaze
(A Symphony of Desire)

The cafe hushes, a witness fades from view,
Café Brulot's flame – a rebellious rendezvous.
Orange liqueur's kiss lingers, a tangy tease,
A promise of pleasure in gentle, heated pleas.

Coffee's earthy musk, a heady brew,
Reflects the primal desires brewing between the two.
Spices like cinnamon and cloves, an aroma that beguiles,
Plant a seed of longing, a hunger for a thousand miles.

Gentle touches ignite, a spark dancing wild,
Clothes flaunting secrets, flames flickering,
beguiled.
Skin on skin brushes, a sensation raw and new,
Café Brulot's intoxicating essence, a script
understood by two.

Lips meet in a searing kiss, a cinnamon fire,
Brandy's warmth floods in, a burning, sweet
desire.
Fingers traverse, delineating unseen arcs,
A cacophony of senses, an ardour's fervent
spark.

The café slumbers, a mausoleum of forgotten
sighs,
Brulot's clementine flames, a clandestine muse,
ignite illicit ties.
Within this hushed alcove, a feral tango unfolds
in the gloaming,
Two souls ignite a conflagration of passion,
aching for uninhibited blooming.

Each touch, a jolt of electricity's fire,
Coffee's bitter edge, a counterpoint, sharp and
higher.
Orange liqueur's sweetness lingers on their
tongues,

Renegade rumba, a rebellious waltz, defying
every right and wrong.

The room shrinks into their cocoon, a haven of
heat,
Café Brulot's glow reflected in their pounding
heartbeat.
Groans and gasps fill the air, a melody unbound,
Lost in a world of their own, in hushed sweet,
primal sound.

As embers wane, a solitary ember persists,
A visceral imprint upon their skin, yearning
eternally kissed.
By the inky cloak of night, Café Brulot's
alchemical might,
A conflagration of longing, where two kindred
spirits take flight.

Irish Coffee's Elixir
(Love's Burning Brew)

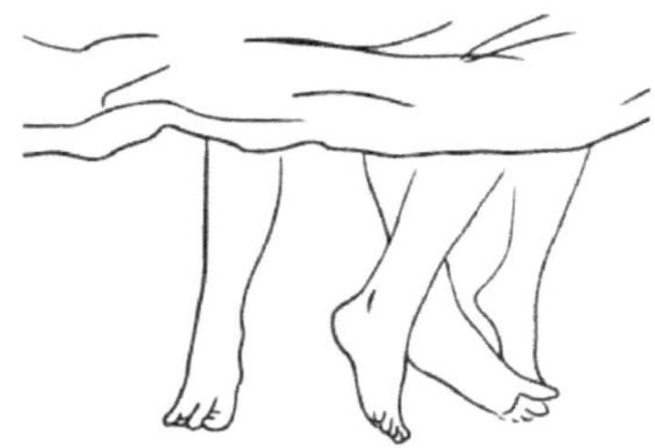

Wispy tendrils ascend, Irish coffee's warm caress,
A sugared brush, flushing a blushing distress upon their cheeks.
With trembling touch, a tendril set aflame, surging a current beneath her skin,
Like whiskey's heat, a sweet malaise, a naughty tang where innocence gives in.

Not the first cup, nor the tenth they've shared with delight,
Each sip ignites a spark, a desire burning ever so bright.
Skin alights where fingertips graze, a fire that sets them ablaze,
Lost in a world of their own, an amazing, captivating maze.

Naked souls amalgamated, a primaeval truth laid
bare,
Palms slick with fervour, like talons tearing
through the silken snare.
Sinuous vows imprinted on alabaster skin, a
cartography by hands,
Love's conflagration, a searing sigil, describing
volcanic lands.

Irish coffee, an intangible chronicle brewed rich
and firm,
Two souls docked, where laughter forever
lingers long.
Living future, poured clear, like coffee in a glass
crystal hold,
A candle burning brighter, a haven built of love
untold.

Irish coffee became their ritual: a shared cup,
morning spark,
A coated memory as the day faded, leaving its
mark.
The aroma, a reminder of treasured secrets and
sparkly glances,
A twirly story brewing in the steamy, swirling
dances.

The time, like aged whiskey, has mellowed their pace,
A depth of understanding carved on each loving face.
Smile paints laughter lines, a map of snapshots made,
Their fondness, like Irish coffee, a comforting cascade.

Cortado Compass
(A Shared Adventure)

Sunlight spills gold across the kitchen's shared
domain,
Where countless mornings bloomed, a
partnership's refrain.
The grinder hums, a metallic rhythm of coffee
beans,
The espresso wishes a dark farewell as the night
leans.

Milk froths to life, a diaphanous embrace,
Emblem of whispered joy, a zephyr's gentle
grace.
The elixir of dawn entices, a perfect, steamy
blend,
A daily chalice where their cognition ascends.

Maps sprawl on the table, worn and creased with
pride,
Each coffee stains a memory, where adventures
confide.
Mountain peaks beckon, a portrait emblazoned
in time,
Together they'll conquer, with hearts and wills
aligned.

Days spent trekking, muscles taut with every
stride,
Burning yet soaring, hearts forever side by side.
Creamy sunsets paint the sky in fiery hues,
The campfire crackles, casting amber views.

Cortado steams in enamel mugs, a shared
delight,
Stars shimmer above, bathing their chit-chat in
soft moonlight.
Moons wax and wane, a calendar evolves its
tale,
Where sandy crescents proclaim, with teeming
stories to exhale.

Turquoise waters crash on pristine shores,
verdant,
A rhapsody on sun-kissed sand.
Seashells hold Cortados, a sweet, salty sip,

As the ocean murmurs secrets, secrets the waves
can't keep.

Though the cartography of their lives expands,
Each shared experience, a fresh inscription
penned.
Cortado mornings, a constant, a companion of
seasons,
A spiritual brew, where ideas are born and move
horizons.

Pour-Over Pain
(Brewing the Vulnerability)

Evening descends, painting the room in a gentle
hue,
Pour-over's gentle murmur, a reverie coming
true.
Water boils, anticipation hangs in the air,
Memories surface, burdens they choose to share.

Fragile aromas waft like haunting steam,
Tears fall like rain, cleansing a long-held dream.
Childhood shadows, shared in hushed tones,
Past relationships' scars, no longer alone.

Bare souls laid naked, bathed in the soft
lamplight,
Vulnerability brewed, a bond taking flight.
Coffee grounds, like hidden flavours, they softly
impart,

Slowly revealed, a buried treasure, under the
clast.

Family's lighthouse, a shelter from the storm,
Now adrift and hopeless, adrift and feeling torn.
Societal expectations, a burden they both knew,
Dreams crushed by judgement, a shared,
unspoken rue.

He speaks of a past where hope was a distant
star,
She roars of battles, scars that mark who they
are.
As each narrative blooms, a prism refracts their
view,
Their realities reflected a trauma dispelled.

In shared tears and unspoken empathy,
They find solace in this newfound intimacy.
Society's harsh whiplashes fade into the night,
Replaced by understanding, a beacon burning
bright.

Pour-over's patience, a metaphor for their
journey's tone,
As healing commences, a bond fully honed.
Steaming compassion, a comforting brew,
Words of acceptance, tucked in soft and true.

The burdens they bore, a shared chalice they pour,
Pasts confessed; a thousand wounds begin to close.
Pour-over's gentle cascade, a ritual that binds their souls,
A shared alchemy ignites; a broken wing unfurled and arose.

Flat White's Saga
(A Year Together)

The air hums with comfort, a year now gently brewed,
Two hearts entwined, a promise steadfast and true.
Walls adorned with memories, each painting a scene,
A chorus of laughter, where joy's the unseen sheen.

The bitterness of past shadows fades with each sunrise,
Replaced by the warmth of shared smiles and loving sighs.
Gleaming candles pierce the cake, like love grooving in the zest,
Family's embrace, a hearth's warm glow, a bond forever best.

Strolling hand-in-hand, a familiar, comforting pace,
Building a refuge, a heart-filled, sacred space.
Furniture holds stories, lulled in gentle chimes,
Pillow fights erupt in shrieks of laughter through jubilant times.

Camaraderie blossoms, a mosaic complete and sewn,
Two destinies intertwine, a singular consciousness known.
Mirth erupts in cascades, narratives exchanged with glee,
This habitat they've forged, a connection defying day flee.

Espresso's robust heart, a bond resolute and true,
Steamed milk's silky blend, a tenderness shining through.
In each sip they share, a blanket of heartfelt vow,
Crafted with passion, forever, here and now.

Disagreements trembled, voices laced with concern,
Yet patience and understanding – a lesson they'd learned.
They learned each other's cadences, a parry and thrust, a flirtatious fray,

Blending like frothed milk and stormy skies, a
love tragical astray.

The flat white's porcelain shroud, a monument
so cold,
Encapsulates the day's embers, a story yet
untold.
Through echoes of boisterous joy and whispers
of despair,
Their souls, like twin flames, forever stamped, a
pair.

Cold Brew's Pause
(Love on Hold)

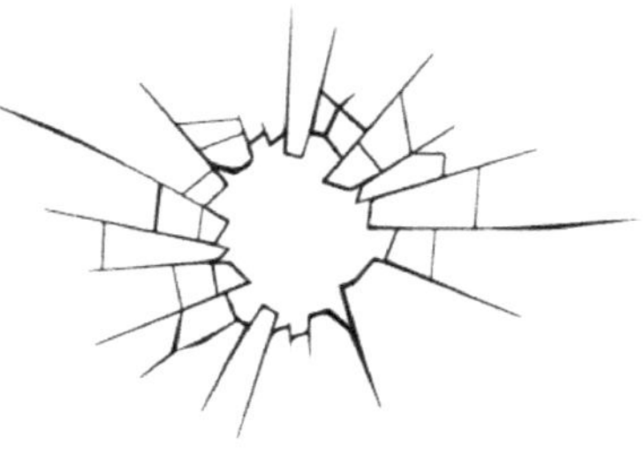

Laughter fills the air as they share a morning
kiss,
Plans for the future and shared promises of bliss.
But a shadow tremored, a weight on their hearts
unseen,
A call they both dread, shattering the world they
have been in.

The news simmers, a bitter aftertaste in the
brew,
Duty's harsh decree, a future cut in two.
Miles stretch before them, a vast and empty
space,
A year of loving tales, replaced by a tear-stained
face.

The cold brew's chill, a metaphor for their fear,
Anxiety's grip tightening, a future unclear.
College binds her, a dream she can't forsake,
His duty calls, a path he's forced to take.

The night, once a comfort, now feels heavy and
still,
Griefs unspoken bloom, a shared and wounding
chill.
Desperate they huddle, sobs racking their frame,
Fear a serpent coiling, hissing a loveless name.

'What will we do'? she questions softly, a touch
of fear in her eye,
He strokes her hair gently, a tethered, starlit tie.
'We'll find a way', he murmurs, voice thick with
emotion,
'Long distance, calls, letters, a bridge defying
the ocean'.

Ceramic fading mirth, a mournful knell
descends,
Their shared euphoria, like an antiphonal
memory that never ends.
Though shadows of trepidation deeply reside,
A glimmer of hope still burns deep inside.

Patience fosters the cold brew, its essence soon
to bloom,
So too their connection, defying the encroaching
tomb.
The wait, a bitter trial, a hurdle they'll consume,
Their bond, a complex aroma, fills every empty
room.

Espresso Sting
(A Bittersweet Farewell)

Suitcases line the floor, a stark reminder of
goodbyes,
Each item he places – a teardrop in disguise.
Her favourite books, a chocolate she adores,
A playlist of her songs, synchronising at each
door.

He tucks away memories in every hidden fold,
A desperate attempt to keep her heart from
growing cold.
A cloying vapour, a ghost of his scent on the
breeze,
A final testament in this hallowed place of
appease.

The night deepens, painting the world a roasted
bean's hue,
A darkness that reflects the despair, breaking
through.
She sneaks in his drawer, a hidden treasure to
find,
His cherished shirt, a comfort for her grieving
mind.

'Leave your perfume', she ordered, voice
trembling with fear,
'Let your scent linger', a silent plea, ever so
clear.
Enveloped by shadows, their forms merge as
one,
A desperate communion, beneath the cloak of
night begun.

Exchanged kisses, a discordant hymn of parting,
Liquid diamonds spill, a saga of a bond
departing.
'What if you forget me'? her worried eyes softly
inquire,
His answer, a searing kiss, a love forever set
afire.

'Relinquish you'? he cries out, voice raspy with
anguish,
'Without your essence, life itself would be
languish'.
Each encounter a clash, a bitter espresso's
acridity,
Yet their connection, a resilient crema, atop
adversities it clings.

The sunrise arrives, a cruel and unwelcome
guest,
A concentrated espresso shot, putting their will
to the test.
Their fingers brush softly, a final, desperate plea,
Worlds shift and shatter, a tsunami drifting away
the sea.

Though severed, a pact ascends on ethereal
wings,
Their fledgling connection, a star outlasting
twilight's sting.
Across the boundless expanse, their spirits
steadfastly soar,
A destiny intertwined; a mystical expresso
essence pours.

Black Russian Roars (The Hollow Echoes)

The taxi rumbles away, a mnémosynic trace in
the air,
The house stands silent, a weight she can't bear.
His scent lingers faintly in every corner and
nook,
A cruel reminder of a flower, now lost in a
distant book.

Her favourite books, untouched; chocolates lie
forlorn,
The silent playlist mocks her with a melody of a
bygone morn.
Tears stream down her face, a black Russian's
bitter flow,
A hollow, lonely night, a future she doesn't
know.

The phone's shrill ring, a lifeline in the night,
His voice, a warm current, a beacon burning
bright.
'I miss you', he sighs, a desolate moan that
cracks the air,
A Black Russian's lingering warmth, a
phantom's tender snare.

'I can still sense your presence', he teases, a
poignant sting,
'That favourite shirt', he chuckles, a hidden truth
to cling.
A shy blush creeps on her face, a secret she can't
deny,
Holding onto his shirt, a piece of him nearby.

The night deepens, a canvas painted black,
She wraps herself in his shirt, a comfort she can't
lack.
Sobbing into the fabric, his scent fading from the
baft,
The emptiness, a black hole, engulfing all that
was left.

He hangs up the phone, a puppet with strings
now severed,
He joins the crowd, a smile painted thin, barely
observed.

Back in his room, a single tear escapes his eye,
He clutches his pillow, mimicking her nightly
sigh.

Though the path stretches endless, shrouded in
the deepest night,
Their resolute spirit, a Kahlúa's unwavering
might.
Like the Black Russian's blend, confluence, both
acrid and sweet,
They'll find comfort in memories until their
destinies meet.

Macchiato Love
(A Year of Digital Touch)

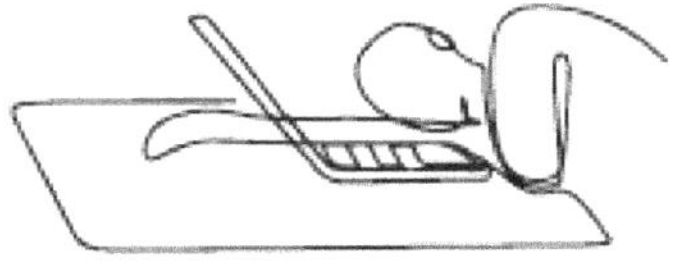

A year elapses, a year apart,
Daily routines scrawled on a digital heart.
Studies consume her, duty binds him tight,
Connection sustained by screens – a pixelated
light.

Sunlight streams in, a familiar routine,
But the empty chair opposite, a laconic, lonely
scene.
Macchiato's frothy nest, a bittersweet tingle,
A lingering echo, a connection that won't
disentangle.

She navigates the cafe, a palimpsest of their
narrative's genesis,
Each nook, a reliquary enshrining fragments of a
love preordained by fate.
Park benches and bookstores stand as stoic,
muted wide,
Smiles like ships that lost their star, adrift on
shifting tides.

Penmanship rumbles on paper, words steeped in ink,
Tears stain the pages, like a soldier drenched in blood.
Late-night calls bridge the distance, voices a soothing balm,
Lullabies sung through screens, fighting with a distance's raging storm.

Distance breeds doubt, a serpent's silent hiss,
Misunderstandings flare, a virtual lovers' kiss.
Patience holds the reins, empathy mends the rift,
Honest words bridge the gap; truth their compass swift.

Across the miles, a palimpsest of the heart in each beat,
He spins tales of her spirit – a bond oh so sweet.
A touch of possessiveness, 'he teases with a wink',
But fiercely loyal, my confidante, a beacon that won't shrink.

Care packages arrive, a tangible token of remembrance,
A knitted scarf, a cherished book, a message from the 'one'.
The physical touch, a distant, burning desire,
Virtual cuddles offered, setting hearts on fire.

Macchiato's fleeting warmth, a fading, bitter dream,
A year in the digital void, their connection's desperate scream.
No screen can mimic skin's embrace; a longing starts to bloom,
A parched vine thirsts for sunlight, reaching past the sterile room.

Nitro Café Surprise
(A Happy Birthday)

Days bled into weeks, a year's slow drip, drip,
drip,
A bitter longing brewing, an obsession on a
lonely ship.
He dreamt of her laughter, the warmth of her
touch,
His fixation, a nitro yearning, a pressure
building too much.

Her birthday loomed, a solitary chime,
Sadness threatened to engulf her, drowning in
the sea of time.
Phone pinged and flooded in, a chorus of empty
cheers,
But her heart ached for one rhyme, that one
voice to hear.

The clock struck twelve, a solemn, lonely beat,
Dew droplets welled in her eyes, a wistful
defeat.
A sudden doorbell's jingle, a melody so bright,
Shattered the night's darkness, a jolt of pure
delight.

Delivery man at the door, bundled up in the
night,
Cakes and flowers in hand – a wondrous,
unexpected sight.
Distracted by greetings, she opened the door
wide,
But a familiar voice exclaimed with delight,
'Happy Birthday, my guide'.

His mask shattered; a storm of emotions took
hold,
A thousand feelings unleashed; a prayer finally
told.
Tears cascaded freely; a dam finally breached,
A flood of memories washed over, a love
unspoken, reached.

He held her close, the feel of her in his arms, a
forgotten utopia,
A renewed energy pulsed – vibrant and devoted
than it would ever seem.
Cake disappeared, laughter filled the air, a wave
of relief washed clean,
Washing away the bitterness, a love's triumphant
hymn.

As night deepened, shy touches turned to sighs,
Gentle touches rekindled beneath moonlit skies.
Depths of intimacy explored, a wellspring to be
drawn from,
The honeycomb full of nectar to be drizzled on.

Night unveiled itself, a nocturnal madrigal of
desire,
A surge of invigorating ardour on thrones
reclaimed by fire.
The acrid sting of estrangement, a spectral
memory now,
Replaced by a rekindled bond fresh as nitro,
vibrant and avow.

Kirsch au Café Promise
(Forever After Coffee)

Morn's dappled fingers reached in, painting their
haven in light,
Kirsch au Café in hand, with stories recounted
through the night.
Their home, once hollow, now held secrets it
would keep,
In each other's arms, morning's warmth was
deep.

Twilight's kiss touched the sky, mirroring the
playful glint in his eyes,
'The pastel green dress', a gracious favour, a
subtle smile tugging at his lips.
Reluctant to part even briefly, she prepared with
tender grace,
Emerging as a vision, beauty lighting up her
face.

Hair flowing like steam, eyes dark as coffee beans,
Lips the hue of cherry brandy, liner sharp in sheen.
He was captivated, breathless at the sight,
She was his vision of perfect light.

The café, their destiny's cradle, adorned in blushing hues,
A sea of peonies awaits, a promise to imbue.
'It must be some event', she fretted with a frown,
But a silent nod from him banished her doubt down.

As her cherished song rippled, memories filled the air,
Lost in the melody, she didn't see him there.
A man in green and black, holding a velvet box tight,
Heart pounding, she questioned if this could be her night.

He knelt and opened the box, a solitaire catching light,
'Will you be my forever, my now, my after, my light'?
Tears filled her eyes, like cherry brandy's melancholic flow,
'Yes'! she cried; love her only guide, aglow.

A joyous roar erupted, loved ones woven in a colourful thread,
Laughter's cascade mingled with tears; a bond triumphantly led.
Solemn vows kissed the air, a future weaved in filigree,
Their destiny, a Kirsch au Cafe's embrace, a sanctum memory to the decree.

Americano Distance
(Miles Between Us)

Another goodbye loomed, a bitter americano brew,
Vacations over, duty called, a promise he had to renew.
This time, the parting sting, sharper than before,
But wedding bells knelled with joy, a joyous promise in store.

Pre-dawn shadows swallowed him whole, a parting shrouded in grief's veil,
A lone crimson bloom remained, a memory in time, frail.
'Eternal love', he vowed, 'My world, prepare to ascend',
'Swift return beckons, to claim you eternally, without end'.

A diaphanous echo of the forty-eight hours
spent,
Love's benediction whispered, a hushed and
sacrosanct descent.
Yet, remembrances, the ephemeral crema's
embrace,
A saccharine counterpoint, a solace in this
mournful space.

Back to screens, they retreated, a digital cup
unfair,
Sharing moments, big and small, a burden they'd
have to bear.
Video calls introduced her to his friends, a
family she'd claim,
But distance gnawed, a constant ache,
murmuring her lover's name.

A whirlwind whipped his days, time a shattered,
fleeting gem,
Yet, an Elysian interlude inscribed a star for her
memory's diadem.
A calming call, a consolation, in duty's
demanding din,
A melancholic serenade on battlefields, where
fate holds them in.

The americano's acrid bite, a stark reminder of
their plight,
Yet, the promise of nuptials, a beacon ablaze
through the darkest night.
Leagues may separate, a song with a bittersweet
strain,
But souls forever tethered, an unyielding refrain.

Decaf Heart
(The Fading Connection)

The world, a centrifuge, flung her towards her
goals' bright spark,
Her internship a crucible, where dreams would
leave their mark.
His training, a sterile cell, a screen his only
friend,
Their messages, once threaded, now a chasm
that yawns wide.

Affection lingered, a low ember in a hearth long
untended,
The warmth waned, starved for the fuel of
shared days suspended.

Conflicting duties drained the well of time, a
precious oasis lost,
Intimacy's fragrance, an indifferent sigh, on a
heart turned to frost.

Their conversations, once lively, felt
decaffeinated and flat,
Short exchanges, a connection lacking that
spark, that chat.
His voice, a hint of tension, a tremor she couldn't
ignore,
But 'I'm fine', he'd always answer, brushing
away the feeling's core.

He felt the strain too, but kept his worries at bay,
Not wanting to burden her in any significant
way.
They both needed more, like coffee craving's
gentle wake,
But time was a thief, stealing moments they
couldn't remake.

She, burdened but determined, pushed worries to
the back of her mind,
Work demanded attention, a task she couldn't
unwind.
But a disquiet settled, a nagging feeling in her
chest,

A lost paradise, a garden waiting for a
long-awaited guest.

The poignant tang of closeness lingered, an
eidolonic echo on her tastebuds,
They ached for the rich, full-bodied elixir; the
vibrant bond now subdued.
Lost in separate voyages, duty's relentless tide
surged high,
A silent undercurrent thrummed; a narrative left
to die.

The behemoth of work, a relentless current,
Hurled them to disparate shores, destinies yet to
be concurrent.
For now, they held onto hope, through the
decaf's quiet plea,
That soon they'd find the time to be together,
finally free.

Lungo Yearning
(A Longing for Connection)

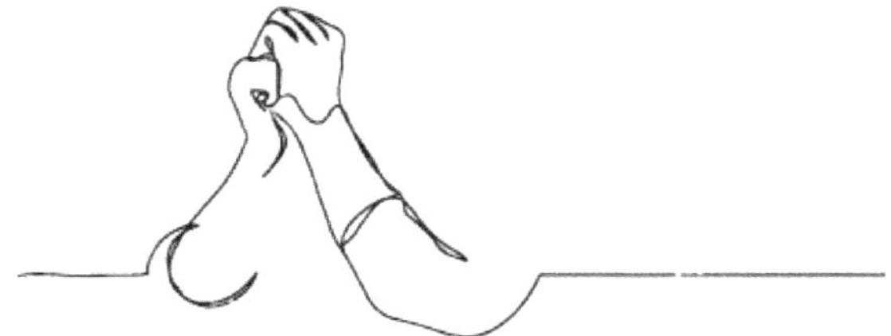

Six months bled into one another, a calendar of
growing nowhere,
Their connection, once vibrant, now a wisp of
smoke in the air.
He, burdened by a secret, a soldier soon to be
shipped afar,
To a war zone's brutal claws, beneath a sky
devoid of a star.

Dire tidings shattered his foundation, dreams
crumbling into ash,
Her visage haunted his thoughts, a bond with a
dubious grasp.
An uncertain horizon distended before him, a
crimson-soaked terrain,
The weight of her potential sorrow, a burden too
heavy to sustain.

Honesty's spectre loomed, a phantom he dared
not confront,
A veil of silence shrouded his family, a loyalty
fraught.
'I'll tell her', he choked out, a lie, a barb in his
throat,
But the fear of her heartbreak, a burden he
couldn't devote.

A twisted masquerade that only he could
conceive,
To cast her adrift, a bitter bulwark against her
tears to receive.
Iced barbs laced his every word, a weapon
forged in despair's hold,
Their incendiary bond, a tapestry now tattered,
waiting to be retold.

The hollowness where he once throbbed in the
night's embrace,
His voice, once a song of solace, now held a
chilling, empty space.
She wove a web of reasons, work's relentless
demands as her plea,
Blind to the truth that festered, a severed bond
set silently free.

He sipped longos of silence, each drop a bitter
decree,
The slow, agonising distance, a torment he
couldn't flee.
The bitterness in his voice, a dark roasted bean's
sting, she felt it too,
A slow unravelling, like pages of a lonely,
mournful book.

Their bond, a wisp of smoke dissolving in the
encroaching night,
Clinging to embers of memory in the dimming,
fragile light.
The abyss yawning between them, a lungo, bitter
and cold,
A spark of defiance flickered within; their story
left on hold.

Red-Eye Mirage
(A Bitter Dark Shot)

Suffocating silence, a shroud of unspoken thralldom,
Espresso pronouncements, bitter and laced with night.
Warmth in his gaze, a shadow forever fled,
A frozen tundra, where their obsolete tale lies dead.

Her heart, a battleground of memories, past hurts that throbbed,
Screaming doubts, a wraith of betrayal shrieked in the void.
'How did we get here'? she'd cry, a question lost in the night,
The warmth of their connection, swallowed by a growing blight.

She clutched the ring he'd given, a promise
crocheted in gold,
But promises seemed like ashes; a pressed
withered rose.
Red-eyed and sleepless, haunted by his cold
replies,
Craving for his touch, a voice that wouldn't
disguise.

Restless nights mirrored his turmoil, solace a
distant dream,
Her laughter, a taunting tune that plays in his
sleepless stream.
Woven justifications crumbled under scrutiny's
harsh glare,
A heavy weight settled in his chest with each
uttered, bitter snare.

Buried in the threadbare folds of his shirt, she
grasped for a spectral anchor,
The redolence of his presence, now shrouded in
secrecy's armour.
A salty waterfall, a heart drowning in torment.
'Hold me', she pleaded to the mirror, 'Tell me
this isn't me'.

The dog-eared passport, a shattered dream's
debris,
Mere hours remain, a frantic bid for hearts to
appease.
His obfuscated form, a stoic observer of her
travail,
Like aeolotropic sands eroding her solace,
dissolving in the exhale.

Red-eyed, spirits wounded, a tethered thread
hangs thin,
Will they mend the broken bridge or forever be
drawn within.
The sepulchral hush, a litany of buried desires,
Can they bridge the fractured covenant or watch
their passion expire?

Empty Cup Residue
(Love Poured Out)

Grim-visaged, a levee of silence cracks,
A deluge of questions pours, truths she yearns to
unlock.
Frantic alacrity propels her towards the venal
exchange,
To confront the deafening void and mend their
sundered circumstance.

A heart weighed down by leaden skies, he
arrived,
To face her, a truth he loathed, a hope
extinguished in her eyes.
He'd donned the shield of confession, a truth
stripped bare and stark,
But at her sight, his resolve splintered, a
desperate tether defying the mark.

The door creaked open, a hesitant greeting, cold
and strange,
Her outstretched hand, a bridge unformed, his
instincts wouldn't arrange.
'What's wrong'? she pleaded, voice trembling
with unshed tears,
'Is it someone else? My love? Or fading,
unspoken fears'?

A leaden hush, a tomb where secrets festered
deep,
Then, a voice, a blade that sliced, where buried
truths now weep.
'It's over', he declared, a verdict sharp and cold,
Shattering her world into pieces, a love story left
enfold.

Numbness settled in, a void where her heart
once resided,
Questions choked back; a dam of emotions
subsided.
The sepia-toned stage, where ghosts of laughter
danced in lorn,
Soft clay, once pliable, hardened in the furnace,
a misshapen form.

With Kintsugi's spirit, a stubborn flame she
fanned,
'Look at me', she challenged him, 'and tell me
you don't feel me'.
At the doorway, they stood, a chasm
unbreachable between,
His gaze locked with hers, a silent, anguished
scene.

He clenched his fists, a strangled cry escaping
his throat,
'I don't', he lied, the words a bitter, choking
note.
A single tear traced a path down her cheek,
glistening bright,
Then, with a nod, she turned away, leaving him
drowning in the night.

The portal slammed shut, a finality etched in the
metallic clang,
He crumbled, a bestial wail reverberating
through the brick walls' domain.
The burden of his affections, a carapace now too
heavy to sustain,
Lost in the bereft of the empty cup, a home
shattered beyond reclaim.

Doppio Nightmare (A Double Shot of Heartbreak)

Doppio's bitter surge, a cold dawn breaks free,
He's far away at war, a soldier meant to be.
Pain for her lingers, a heart disguised in steel,
Duty calls, a leader, emotions he must conceal.

Sleep evaded his grasp, a cruel, bitter jest,
Haunted by two faces, forever impressed.
Her evanescent tip-toe, a susurrus of sorrow that
was born,
He craved the caffè forte's fire to mend his
shattered bones.

The hinges sigh, a mournful tremor in the air,
A disintegrated world, a connection beyond
repair.

A raw howl pierces the void, a soul stripped
bare,
As if a fragment of her essence dissolved in
despair.

Time, a viscous mire, swallows each
monotonous beat,
A prisoner in a gilded cage, where memories are
bittersweet.
A labyrinth of might-have-beens, where faded
dreams convene,
Each corner a memory, a lost piece of heart that
now screams.

Silence pressed in on her, a suffocating weight,
The ring on her finger, a promise turned to hate.
His shirt, a phantom touch, a scent that brought
back pain,
She pushed it away, the memories like a
relentless rain.

The world outside faded, a distant, muted sound,
She retreated inwards, on a battlefield unfound.
No solace in conversation, no comfort in a
friend,
Just a hollow existence, waiting for the bitter
end.

He, too, in an oubliette of sorrow, a prisoner of
the past,
Where solace finds no purchase and memories
forever cast.
A spectral lament, a dirge echoing in the
chambers of his mind,
A stoic pilgrim on a path of thorns, redemption
yet to be found.

Doppio's searing bitterness, a hidden wound they
both concealed,
Two souls lacerated; a vibrant fresco of
connection once revealed.
He, a warrior lost in a wasteland of strife, she, a
ghost in a gilded cage,
Entangled in the wreckage, consumed by an
existence without an age.

Instant Coffee Jitters
(Just a Sip of You)

Two moons have waned, a soldier weathered and
worn,
Tomorrow's dawn, a deployment where hope
seems forlorn.
Beneath a sky where stars withhold their light,
winter's cruel clasp descends,
He huddles low, a veiled enigma – a saga that
transcends.

His thoughts, a labyrinth of memories
tantalising,
Aching for her touch, a refuge from the conflict's
paralysing.
A phantom ember's embers flicker, a memory's
fire to greet,
Her eyes, a starlit sky at twilight, a mystery
unswept.

Her voice, a desolation's dirge, a lament in the
night,
Erasing the anger, the self-inflicted plight.
He craves her touch, her curves, a vision in his
mind,
A comforting cup of instant coffee, the amnesia
he can't find.

He tears open a packet, the hiss a fleeting sigh,
Hot water joins the grounds, a teardrop in his
eye.
The dark liquid swirls, a bitter reflection of his
soul,
'Will I ever be forgiven'? a silent question takes
its toll.

The acrid essence, a memory's caress of her
bygone perfume,
A poignant residue of laughter, once woven with
wispy steam's plume.
He raises the cup to his lips, the bitterness a tidal
wave on his tongue,
A searing reflection of his anguish, a connection
forever unsung.

Sleep, a stolen solace, a warmth his body
yearned to reclaim,
Imprints of her touch, a bond he fiercely sought
to rekindle's flame.

Two gunshots shatter the dream, a harsh reality's
sting,
Back to the inferno of war, where life and death
take wing.

He rises, a warrior rechristened, duty's iron yoke
upon his form,
But in his heart, an ember persists, a yearning
refusing to conform.
For if fate grants him a reprieve, bathed in the
sun's celestial grace,
He'll surge toward her, their broken accord a
relentless, desperate chase.

Tangled limbs, whispered dreams, a haven
they'd meticulously forge,
A familial symphony, a vision held aloft in the
steam's surge.
Broken might but a burning desire to heal his
world's wounded face,
The soldier fights on, fuelled by a promise
whispered in that instant's space.

Nightcap Tears
(Wish You Were Here)

The house, once like mother's arms, now a
suffocating cage,
Memories clung to the walls, turning every page.
Boxes piled high, a dirge of farewells sung,
Thick with unspoken words, a weight upon her
lungs.

His shirt, a haunting reminder, a wisp of
memory on the breeze,
The fading perfume, a silver exhalation of
moments of ease.
She held it close, a fragile barrier against a
gaping wound,
A treasured memento, a bond tragically
unwound.

The phone, a constant companion, a silent,
mocking friend,
Each check, a desperate plea, an unrequited
deed.
Was it a gilded cage, the laughter, a
mockingbird's mimicry?
Did his promised solace wither, marking a lost
territory?

Tonight, the final excision of a connection
turned crystalline,
His barren expanse of the sheets, a saga eternally
confined.
A hand probes the air, a spectral imprint in the
vacancy,
'The hunger for the solace of his touch, a
yearning eternally free'.

'Comb my fingers through your hair', a
memory's sweet sting,
'Tell me your stories; make my heart take wing'.
His embrace, a sheltering oak, where tempests
dared not revoke,
Now stands a skeletal bough, where memories
whisper and bow.

The Nightcap coffee, A comforting potion,
keeping secrets a deal,
Dark, roasted depths hold a velvety rhyme,
another turn of the wheel.
It soothes the tongue, as gyrating emotions begin
to take hold,
A hand wraps the mug, a shield from the storm,
where tears unfold.

A meticulously woven vision, unravelled by
fate's callous touch,
A spectral brood, dreams of children dissolved
in the relentless slush.
A convulsive sob shattered the stillness, a
tempest in her weary soul,
Clinging to embers of a future extinguished,
promises lost in a desolate hole.

She agitates the libation, a maelstrom of colours
in the muted glow,
A kaleidoscope of emotions, imprisoned in a
labyrinthine throe.
With each imbibing, a recollection unearthed, a
bittersweet mélange,
The final nightcap, as the tempestuous rain
strums its dirge's range.

Affogato Façade
(The Half-Waking Drown)

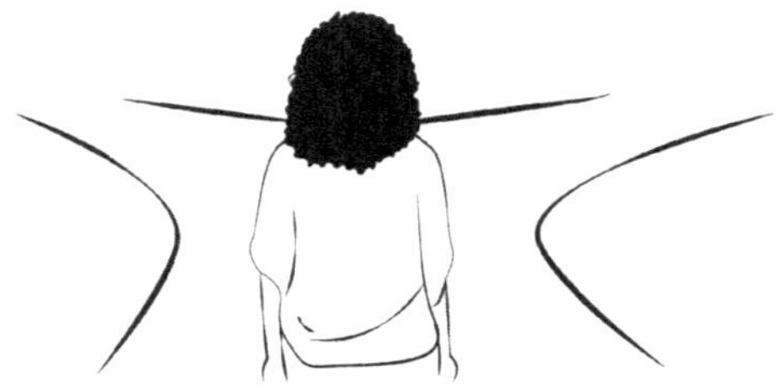

Dawn's icy grip tightens on the shattered pane,
A cold dread curdles in her chest, a burden to
sustain.
Cardboard coffins, stoic sentinels of dreams
turned to ash,
A dirge of goodbyes rises from a life's pyre – a
desolate last splash.

The long-forsaken garment, memory's display,
Held phantasmagoria of touches, a bygone day.
A teardrop traced a path, a glistening streak,
On the worn cotton, his name, soft, but not
weak.

With trembling hands, she handed over the keys,
A young couple waiting, oblivious to the
memories.
A single check, a forced smile, a final goodbye,

Driving away from the past, with a tear in her
eye.

Within the sterile confines of her new abode, the
coffee maker thrummed,
An ethereal tendril of roasted essence, slowly
overcoming the numb.
The obsidian depths of the black nectar, a
steadfast friend on the window pane,
A silent observer of her time, like seconds' hand
on a clock's vertical plane.

She poured it over ice cream, a swirl of white
and brown,
A turbulent mixture, mirroring her upside down.
A rictus grin, a charade for the public gaze,
Like the affogato's juxtaposed sensations, a
bitter blaze.

In the mirror's cold gaze, an alien form took
hold,
A fragment cleaved from her core, a void left
unfilled and cold.
The ghost of a smile refused to bloom, a tempest
in her soul's embrace,
A resonant void reverberated; a war waged
within this desolate space.

New job, new faces, a hesitant hello,
An affogato smile, a highly practised show.
Espresso's bitter disguise, for the ache that
festers beneath her eyes,
Ice cream's facade, a sugary sheen, masking the
sorrow, a heart unseen.

Nights were for tears, a release in the dark,
Days for laughter, a spark in the park.
Gardening became her solace, a connection to
grow,
Peace sought in nature, letting her spirit flow.

With each tentative tread, a fresco unveils,
Brushstrokes of courage on weathered,
tear-streaked trails.
The affogato, a memory's lingering chill,
Melts on a sun-warmed tongue, a promise to
fulfill.

Ristretto Mists
(A Lingering Aftertaste)

Three months had passed, a slow climb out of
despair,
But tonight, sleep was a distant, forbidden affair.
His thoughts, a tidal wave, crashing down in the
night,
She rose, seeking peace in the pale moonlight.

Drawn to a hidden drawer, a treasure she kept,
The light blue shirt, his fragrance, a memory
unslept.
Trembling hands unfolded the fabric so worn,
Searching for comfort, a remnant to be born.

The perfumed promise soured, a cruel and
mocking jest,
The ristretto she brewed, a bitter tang that
wouldn't rest.
Potent draught, an icy grip of an unforgiving
past,
A shade of warmth lingers, an empty wall where
shadows cast.

At 4 a.m., restlessness seeps in, a hollow feeling,
A warmth envelops her, a touch from within.
As if he's there, hands holding hers tight,
A kiss on her forehead, comforting her night.

Her lips quivered, a yearning so deep,
But a strange calm washed over her, a peace in
her sleep.
Tears wouldn't fall, replaced by a quiet surprise,
A slumber descended, with a weight lifted from
her eyes.

Sunlight streamed through, chasing away the
night,
Her gaze fell upon the garden, a breathtaking
sight.
A crimson flower bloomed, a radiant surprise,
His favourite flower, a whole ocean, welled in
her eyes.

The ristretto sat untouched, a forgotten brew,
Unbeknownst to her, the news announced to the
crew.
His name, a weight upon the stone, a soldier's
burden bravely borne,
Three bullets stole his youthful breath, a
sacrifice made exactly at 4 a.m.

Daybreak's veil stretched, a canvas of blissful
unawareness,
His kin, burdened by a truth shrouded in quiet
duress.
She steeled herself, a fractured life to
reconstruct,
The ristretto, a bitter pang, a soul forever
defunct.

The ristretto, a sun-bleached photograph, details
blurring in the dust,
Bitter and short-lived, a memory that stubbornly
refuses to rust.
His absence, a constant ache, a herculean burden
upon her core,
In slumber's embrace, in rustling leaves, a
presence she can't ignore.

Bulletproof Ground
(Love's Armoured Fight)

Years spun a web of triumphs, bulletproof and grand,
Boardroom battles won; victories remarked in sand.
Laughter rings in her office, a life vibrant and bright,
Yet, a corner of her heart held onto a fading light.

The scarlet bloom returned, a beacon bathed in sun,
A silent elegy, a memory on the run.
But today, a knock shattered the serene facade,
A stranger at the door, a storm where calm had laid.

'Is this bulletproof'? the woman asked, a
questing question of the nexus,
A white-hot shock hit her; a world stopped on its
axis.
'Bulletproof'? she thrums, the question a shard
in her throat,
He'd extol that name, a battle cry he'd emote, a
wartime wife he'd devote.

Bound by the iron grip of fate, he shielded me
from the maelstrom at the war,
His heart but always a soul's compass, longing
for his north pole star.
'Your name, a constellated prayer on his final
quest', she jitters,
'A love that lingered, a defiance against death's
tightest fetters'.

A worn address, a fresco done in fading ink,
'You were his love', the woman's hushed voice
did think.
The truth, a cruel sledgehammer, stole the air
from her chest,
A shared illusion shattered; a future laid to rest.

A steely vapour ascends, a dirge of bitterness in
her cup,
An ache of absence lingers, a toll emotionally
wrung up.

Achievements a mirage, a fortress built on brittle ground,
His boast of 'bulletproof' now a twisted, mocking sound.

The bulletproof elixir, a strange and pungent potion,
Coils within her belly, a mirroring disquiet's notion.
But within her, a strength, a heart that learned to cope,
Carrying the memory, with a sip from her bulletproof hope.

The word 'bulletproof' hung in the air, a spectral plea of his vanished hold,
A reminder of her own strength, a phoenix rising in fires like gold.
She looked at the woman, a shared tear they would mend,
Two lives touched by him, a tangled web that wouldn't bend.

The Last Sip Whispers
(Echoes in the Empty Cup)

In time's grand orchestration, we stand as
singular notes,
Woven with the world's vast rondo, yet
harbouring our own tones.
No triumphant heroes crowned, nor vanquished
left to lament,
Life's intricate shelf accumulates, with each
experience, a fragment.

Joy's vibrant pageant, with the sun's descent,
begins to dim,
Sorrow's sting, a spectral echo, a memory yet to
hymn.
Pain's jagged blade, by time's gentle touch, finds
its sharpness subdued,
Even laughter, that transient visitor, once
ardently pursued.

Life's protracted journey presents an endless
throng,
Each leaving indelible marks where burdens
once belonged.
We share a fragment, a fleeting moment, a
respite from the load,
But ultimately, a treasured remnant, a cherished
spark bestowed.

Untarnished by life's tempests, a core of purity
remains,
An essence within, impervious to existence's
bitter strains.
Like a ruby jewel adorning a decadent tier,
This sweetest essence, a solace we hold ever
near.

We yearn to decipher meaning, for love's
quintessential light,
A fervent desire to grasp its essence, ever
burning bright.
Born not merely to exist but to offer and partake,
With hearts unveiled, a love that transcends
compare.

My constant companion, a steaming chalice of
brew,
Witnesseth life's grand tapestry, emotions ever
true.
Each imbibing, a microcosm, a universe
contained,
Dark, enigmatic depths, where strength is yet
unchained.

The creamy crest, a sweetness delicate and
bright,
Invigorates the senses, granting us a clearer
sight.
The final sip, it holds the most profound weight,
As emptiness reminds us of life's impermanent
state.

For when abundance prevails, our vision may
grow dim,
But the final essence, a sage's gift, sets our spirit
free within.
The sweetness lingers, serene and crystal clear,
In the culmination, what remains is truly held
most dear.

Degust each nectareous effusion as life's tide
waxes and wanes,
Engulf yourself in the maelstrom, where time's
grand narrative reigns.

With fortitude, await the final draft; let life's essence unfold,
For in the last sip, its most profound truths are extolled.